Barry Sanders

by Mark Stewart

ACKNOWLEDGMENTS
The editors wish to thank Barry Sanders for his cooperation in preparing this book.
Thanks also to Integrated Sports International for their assistance.

PHOTO CREDITS
All photos courtesy AP/Wide World Photos, Inc. except the following:

Vince Manniello/Sports Chrome – cover
Oklahoma State University – 4 top left, 22 bottom left, 40 top left
Barry Sanders – 9, 12, 18 bottom
Mark Stewart – 48

STAFF
Project Coordinator: John Sammis, Cronopio Publishing
Series Design Concept: The Sloan Group
Design and Electronic Page Makeup: Jaffe Enterprises, and
       Digital Communications Services, Inc.

LIBRARY OF CONGRESS CATALOGING-IN-PUBLICATION DATA
Stewart, Mark.
    Barry Sanders / by Mark Stewart.
       p. cm. – (Grolier all-pro biographies)
    Includes index.
    Summary: Covers the personal life and football career of the well-known running back for the
Detroit Lions.
    ISBN 0-516-20139-5 (lib. binding)–ISBN 0-516-26001-4 (pbk.)
    1. Sanders, Barry, 1968-   –Juvenile literature. 2. Football players–United States–Biography–
Juvenile literature. [1. Sanders, Barry, 1968-   . 2. Football players. 3. Afro-Americans–Biography.]
I. Title. II. Series.
GV939.S18S84 1996
796.332'092–dc20
    [B]   96-5105
                                                                                                            CIP
                                                                                                            AC

Grolier **ALL-PRO** *Biographies*™

Barry Sanders

by
Mark Stewart

CHILDREN'S PRESS®
A Division of Grolier Publishing
New York • London • Hong Kong • Sydney
Danbury, Connecticut

Contents

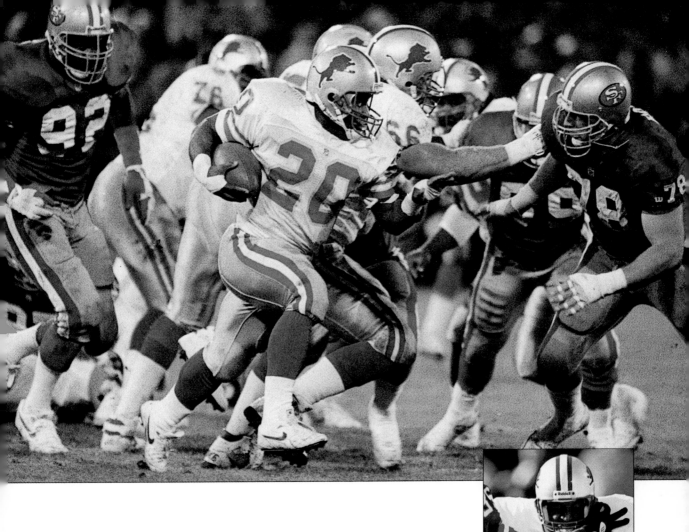

Who

Am I?

Football players come in all shapes and sizes. Some are tall and fast, while others are large and powerful. Some, like me, aren't very big at all. Of course, by the time I reached the NFL I was used to being the tiniest player on the field. Ever since the fourth grade I had been a lot smaller than other children my age. Today, most of my teammates are eight or nine inches taller than I am, and some outweigh me by more than 100 pounds! What I discovered is that there is a place for a little man in a big man's game. The size of your body is not as important as the size of your heart. My name is Barry Sanders, and this is my story . . . "

"There is a place for a little man in a big man's game."

Growing

Barry Sanders grew up in Wichita, a city in the southern part of Kansas. He had eight sisters and two brothers. Barry's father was a carpenter and his mother spent most of her time taking care of the kids. His parents set very high standards for their children and ran a strict household. Barry appreciated how hard his parents worked, and he admired his mother for returning to college so she could become a nurse.

When he was young, Barry struggled in school. He found that he had to work harder than most of the other kids just to keep up. He found science and English most difficult, but by putting in extra study time, he managed to get good grades. The toughest thing for Barry was getting his homework done. With all his brothers and sisters running around the house, it wasn't easy to find a quiet place to study.

Barry really began to enjoy school in the third grade. His teacher that year was Miss Boyd. With the permission of Barry's parents, she kept him after school and gave him challenging

Up

assignments. At first, he did not see the point of doing extra work, but later he came to appreciate her interest in his studies.

Barry had an extra reason to make sure his grades were good. The rule in the Sanders home was "no homework, no sports." Not being able to play sports would have been a tough punishment for Barry to endure because he loved sports from an early age. When he was eight years old, Barry watched the United States basketball team win a gold medal in the 1976 Olympics. The stars of the team were Adrian Dantley and Walter

Barry and his father

Davis. Barry was so excited by the Olympic basketball team that he decided he wanted to be a famous basketball star. He had been playing basketball since he was six years old, and already he could jump much higher than other children his age.

Barry was also a football player, even though he was shorter and smaller than most of his friends. He and his friends played a game called "cream the carrier," or "keep away." In this game, the person with the football must keep running until he is brought down by the other players. Because Barry was too little to overpower the other kids, he learned to twist and turn and spin and squirm. These are the same moves he uses to elude tacklers today.

Barry remembers, "My most embarrassing moment happened when I was in fifth grade. I was one of the smaller players on the team and my pants were a little too big for me. I was returning a kickoff when my belt came loose and, well, I kind of lost my pants! I stopped running and just hit the ground—I didn't care about a touchdown, I just wanted to pull my pants back up!"

Barry, his brothers, and his father were big football fans. On Sundays, after the Sanders family returned from church,

Barry and his brothers would watch NFL games on television. He especially enjoyed seeing running backs Terry Metcalf, Joe Washington, Greg Pruitt, and Tony Dorsett, each of whom was under six feet tall. But Barry's favorite player was Billy Sims, an All-American running back for the University of Oklahoma, who played his football on Saturdays.

When he was young, Barry's football heroes included "Little" Joe Washington of the Redskins (left) and Tony Dorsett of the Dallas Cowboys (right).

The new "20" and the old "20" are worn by Barry Sanders and Billy Sims.

Barry recalls, "In 1978, Sims scored 20 touchdowns and was awarded the Heisman Trophy as America's best college player. He became an NFL star with the Detroit Lions and wore number 20. When I was drafted by the Lions, they gave me the number 20 jersey. What an honor that was!"

As Barry got older, many of his friends began experimenting with alcohol and drugs. Barry and his brother, Byron, decided the smartest thing to do on weekends was to pass up the parties and head over to the high-school stadium. There they ran up and down the steps, building their strength and stamina while staying clear of trouble. The extra workouts helped. By the time Barry enrolled at North High School, he had become an excellent athlete.

When he was 15 years old, Barry made the varsity football team. He wanted to play running back, but the coach thought he was too small. Barry decided that was okay because the team's top runner was his older brother, Byron. Barry did not want to compete with his own brother for the position. Playing behind Byron, Barry did not get a chance to carry the ball until his senior season. Then, in his first game at running back, Barry showed his coaches what they had been missing—he scored four touchdowns and gained 274 yards!

Barry was a good student throughout high school, but today he thinks he should have worked even harder. "I wish I had applied myself a little more when I was in school, not in any particular subject, but in everything. My grades were okay, but I could have worked much harder. I know now that the harder you work, the better you get at whatever you do. And I have found that there is always a way to work harder. Of course, everything begins with reading. It is so very important. You also need to develop writing and math skills. You have to have a good grasp of the fundamentals before you can be successful at anything."

College

Barry Sanders received scholarship offers from four nearby universities: Wichita State, Iowa State, Tulsa University, and Oklahoma State. He knew the chances of a career in pro-football were poor for a player his size, so he wanted to make sure that he got a good education. With help from his parents,

Barry chose Oklahoma State, which they felt offered the best business program. Barry's father warned him, "Don't dare come back here in four years high-fiving and hollering about what you have done on some football field. Come back with a job and an education."

Barry took his father's advice and studied hard in college.

Years

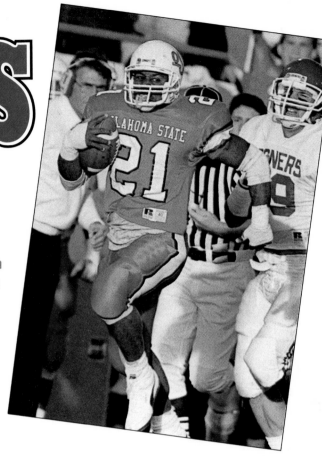

Barry breaks away from the pack for one of his many touchdowns at Oklahoma State.

At Oklahoma State, Barry did well in his studies and enjoyed his time in the classroom. But he was not having such a great time on the football field. For two years, he was a backup to Oklahoma State's top runner, Thurman Thomas. During that time, Barry watched and learned, and he also gained valuable experience returning kickoffs. He was so good that in 1987 he led the nation with an average of 31.6 yards per return. What he wanted most of all, however, was a chance to start at running back.

arry finally got that chance in 1988 and he was incredible. He carried the ball more times and for more yards than any runner in the country. He scored 37 touchdowns, which also led the nation. Barry was a unanimous choice for All-America honors and was the hands-down winner of the Heisman Trophy. Everyone was amazed by Barry's season. How could such a little guy put up such huge numbers? What records would he break in his final season?

Little did they know that Barry would never play another down for the Oklahoma State Cowboys.

A look at Barry's college stats shows how he improved each year

AVERAGE YARDS PER CARRY

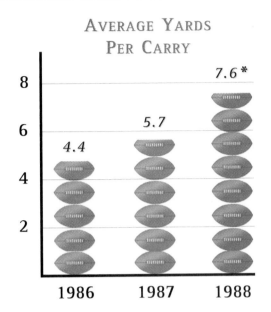

1986	1987	1988
4.4	5.7	7.6*

*Led nation

RUSHING TOUCHDOWNS

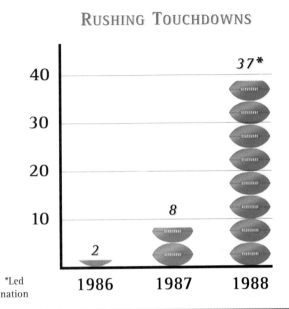

1986	1987	1988
2	8	37*

Barry sets the single season rushing record against Texas Tech on December 4, 1988. Here, he breaks one for 58 yards.

In 1988, Barry led all college running backs with 37 rushing touchdowns.

After winning the Heisman Trophy, Barry discussed his future with his coach, Pat Jones (right). Barry decided to enter the NFL.

Barry's father, mother, and brother Byron (left to right) celebrate after Barry won the Heisman Trophy in 1988.

A few weeks after his fantastic 1988 season, Barry received some shocking news. Oklahoma State had broken several rules while recruiting new players, and the school's punishment in 1989 would be severe. The Cowboys' record would not count toward their conference title, their games would not be televised, and they would not be allowed to participate in any of the important bowl games. Worst of all, no matter how well Barry and his teammates played, they would not be considered for the national championship—something Barry wanted very dearly.

Barry asked his parents what he should do. Barry's father said that it was unfair to be punished for something he did not do, and he suggested that Barry leave school and enter the NFL draft. Barry's mother did not want to see her youngest son leave school without a diploma, but she, too, saw little reason to risk a serious injury by playing a season that wouldn't even count. In the end, Barry decided to leave college. In the 1989 NFL draft, he was selected by the Detroit Lions.

The Story

Since joining the Detroit Lions in 1989, Barry Sanders has become one of the greatest runners in NFL history. He is tough, durable, and nearly impossible to tackle one-on-one. And the bigger the game, the better Barry plays. His best performance came on Thanksgiving Day 1991, when millions of football fans across the country watched the Detroit Lions battle the Minnesota Vikings. Barry's team needed a victory to make the playoffs.

During the game, one of Barry's teammates, Mike Utley, suffered an injury to his neck that left him paralyzed. Everyone on the team was very sad and no one felt like finishing the game. But with the season on the line, they knew they had to play on. That is

Continues

when Barry took over. He ran the ball directly into the famous Minnesota defense all day long, piling up a team-record 220 yards and scoring four touchdowns. When the final gun sounded, he had led the Lions to an emotional 34–14 win. With Barry leading the way, Detroit kept right on rolling—all the way to the NFC Championship Game!

Barry had the finest year of his career in 1994, gaining 1,883 yards and averaging 5.7 yards per carry. Both figures led the league and were personal bests for Barry. In 1995, he helped the Lions make the playoffs again with a solid season. Using Barry as a decoy to confuse the defense, Detroit quarterback Scott Mitchell was able to pass for more than 4,000 yards. This dynamic duo went into the record books as the only 1,500-yard runner and 4,000-yard passer to play for the same team in the same season!

Timeline

1988: Sets 13 college records and wins the Heisman Trophy

1989: Drafted by the Detroit Lions

1986: Enters Oklahoma State University

1990: Wins first NFL rushing title

1992: Leads the Lions to the NFC Championship Game

1991: Selected All-Pro for third consecutive season

1994: Wins second NFL rushing title

Game

Many people believe that Barry is the best player the Detroit Lions have ever had. It's hard to disagree. After only six seasons, he had broken nearly every Lions rushing record.

Barry is one of the best leapers in football. His vertical jump was once measured at $41^{1}/_{2}$ inches.

Anybody can make the first guy miss (a tackle) . . . I want to make the second and third guys miss, too."

Action!

"People say my eyes get big right before a run."

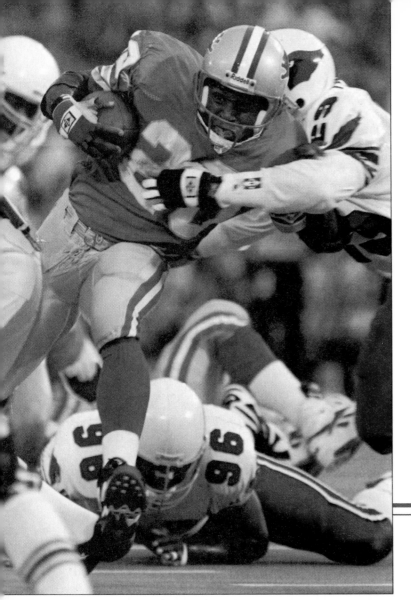

What I do is basically survive . . . If I don't make a guy miss or if I don't outrun him, he's going to do his best to drive me into the ground."

Barry is still standing after running past the entire Cardinals line.

Barry counts his team's 38-6 defeat of the Cowboys in the 1991 playoffs as one of his proudest moments.

In a 1989 game against the Green Bay Packers, Barry was so hard to tackle that the officials actually stopped the game to see if he had sprayed his uniform with a slippery substance called silicone.

Barry has a unique ability to spin out of trouble, and he can change direction without breaking stride. Just when you think you've got him, he's gone!

Dealing

Barry Sanders faced the same tough decisions as most kids. Sometimes he was pressured by his friends to do things he knew were wrong, such as stealing candy or starting fights in school. "I definitely got into some trouble," Barry recalls, "but nothing very serious." But little things can lead to big things—and big trouble. Barry learned this the hard way from his oldest brother, Boyd. Boyd fell in with a rough crowd and often stayed out all night. Eventually, he got into big trouble. Barry saw what might await him if he didn't find a better way to occupy his time, so he decided to dedicate himself to sports. By the way, Boyd eventually straightened out his life. In fact, he became a minister!

With It

Barry sits on the bench during Detroit's 20–10 loss to the Bears in 1994. Barry was held to 42 yards on the ground. The previous week he had gained 237 yards!

How Does

He Do It?

Barry Sanders has been called the "King of the Cutback." A cutback is a move you make when the defense is moving in the same direction you are. If you are moving to the right, plant your right foot and quickly push off in the opposite direction. If you are moving to the left, plant your left foot and do the same. If you have disguised the move properly, the defenders will continue running in the same direction for another step or two before reversing themselves. This gives you a great head start going the other way. What makes Barry so tough to tackle is that just when the defense has switched direction, he'll cut back the *other* way and make them really look silly!

Every year since Barry Sanders arrived in the NFL, he has improved his pass-catching ability. Why would the game's most elusive runner want to get involved in the team's passing attack? Because when a running back goes out for a pass, he is usually covered by a linebacker. The way Barry sees it, if he can get the ball and go one-on-one with a linebacker, he is going to win that battle almost every time. If a quicker defensive back comes over to help, that means one of Detroit's other receivers will have just one man to beat for a big gain.

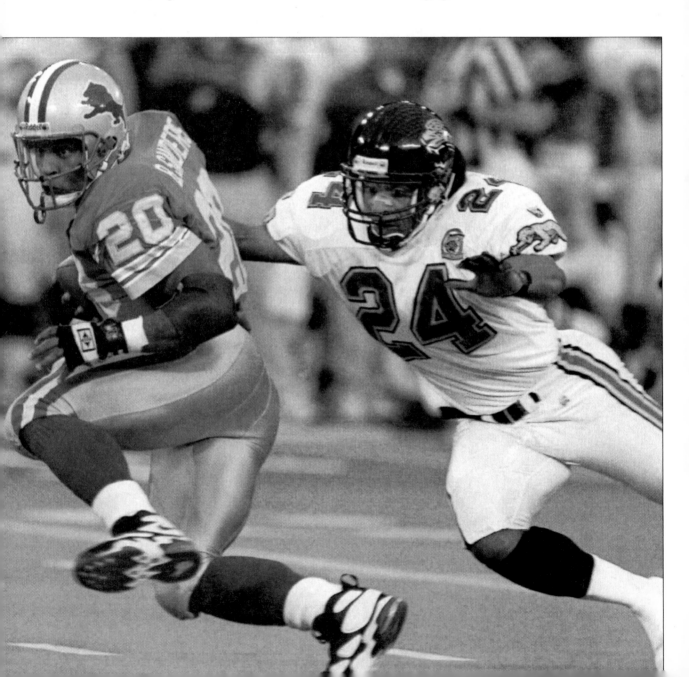

Barry has worked hard to become a top-notch receiver.

Barry says, "I've worked especially hard on my pass-receiving skills. I think I've improved quite a bit, but I know I can still get better."

The Grind

Barry Sanders is in constant demand. He tries to honor as many requests as he can for interviews and appearances, but if he said yes to everyone there would be no time left to play football! The one place Barry will not appear is at a card collecting show. Early in his career, he thought card shows would be a great way to meet the fans, but he was heartbroken when he found out that little kids were paying $20 for his signature. Barry still signs autographs, but he doesn't charge for it.

"The hardest thing about being a professional athlete is trying to protect your privacy. It also makes me uncomfortable when I have people coming up and screaming my name as though I'm a god. I really don't like that part of my success."

Barry sometimes feels uncomfortable being a public star, but he still makes as many public appearances as he can. Here he is presented with an award from heavyweight champion George Foreman.

Family

Barry Sanders is not married, but he has plenty of family. His parents, William and Shirley, still live in Wichita. Barry visits them as often as he can during the off-season. He talks to his sisters—Ardalia, Helen, Nancy, Gloria, Donna, Gina Marie, Elissa, and Krista—all the time. Many of them have started families of their own, and Barry enjoys playing uncle to his new nephews and nieces. He is also close to his older brothers, Byron and Boyd.

Barry celebrates his Heisman Trophy with his mother and father. Barry is not married, but he has lots of family—two brothers and eight sisters!

Matters

Say What?

Here's what football people are saying about Barry Sanders:

"I don't know if I was ever that good."

—*Walter Payton,
Hall of Fame running back*

"There have been times when I knew I had him . . . and I tackled air."

—*Bill Bates, Dallas Cowboys safety*

"He has the most unusual ability to stop and start that I've ever seen."

—Dan Henning, former Detroit Lions offensive coordinator

"His legs go in fourteen different directions at one time."

*—Tim Goad,
Cleveland Browns nose tackle*

"He's like a little sports car."

*—Trace Armstrong,
veteran defensive end*

Career

Among the 13 NCAA records Barry set in his final season at Oklahoma State were 37 rushing touchdowns and 3,250 total yards. He is one of only six college juniors to win the Heisman Trophy.

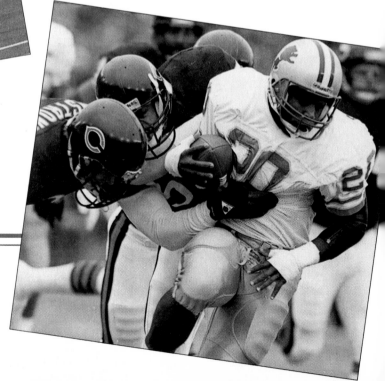

Barry drags Chicago Bears tacklers on his way to becoming Rookie of the Year in 1989.

Highlights

I n 1989, Barry rushed for 1,470 yards and was selected NFL Rookie of the Year. His incredible running helped the lowly Lions win six of their last seven games.

B arry led the NFL with 1,883 rushing yards in 1994. Only three other players in NFL history have gained more yards in a season.

Barry has played in the Pro Bowl every year of his career except 1994, when he declined the invitation because of a painful injury.

Reaching

For the last few years, Barry Sanders has been the "go-to guy" as far as Michigan's Special Olympians are concerned. He has gotten involved in a successful fund-raising program called "Barry Sanders Pay-By-Play." Barry asks all of his fans to pledge a penny for every yard he gains during the season. At the end of the year, all of the money goes to the Oakland County Special Olympics. The money helps pay for new equipment for disabled athletes involved in the Special Olympics. Needless to say, there are a lot of very special kids pulling for Barry on each and every play.

Out

Among other charities, Barry is a member of Athletes for Abstinence. The group tells kids how to make better choices in their relationships. Above (left to right), Darrell Green (Washington Redskins), Barry, David Robinson (San Antonio Spurs), and A. C. Green (Phoenix Suns) record a song called "It Ain't Worth It" for the group.

Numbers

Name: Barry Sanders

Born: July 16, 1968

Height: 5' 8"

Weight: 205 pounds

Uniform Number: 20

College: Oklahoma State University

Barry topped 1,000 rushing yards in each of his first seven seasons. He and all-time great Eric Dickerson are the only players ever to accomplish this feat.

Year	Team	Games	Carries	Yards	Average	Catches	TDs
1989	Detroit Lions	15	280	1,470	5.8	24	14
1990	Detroit Lions	16	255	1,304*	5.1	36	16*
1991	Detroit Lions	15	342	1,548	4.5	41	17*
1992	Detroit Lions	16	312	1,352	4.3	29	10
1993	Detroit Lions	11	243	1,115	4.6	36	3
1994	Detroit Lions	16	331	1,883*	5.7*	44	8
1995	Detroit Lions	16	314	1,500	4.8	48	11
Totals		105	2,077	10,172	4.9	258	79

* Led League

What If...

Being a professional athlete doesn't make me better than anyone. It just makes me luckier. What if I had not been lucky, and something had prevented me from playing football? I'd like to think I would be the same person with the same convictions. As for a profession, I like to work with my hands, so I would probably do something along those lines, like my father. He was a carpenter, a roofer, and a home repairman while I was growing up. I think I could be happy doing that, too. The business courses I took in college would come in handy for keeping the books and running the business."

Glossary

CONVICTIONS the moral principles and rules one believes in and lives by

DECLINED turned down; said no

DECOY a person or object that leads others into a trap

ABSTINENCE stopping oneself from doing things, such as drinking, that are tempting but harmful; self-control

CONSECUTIVE several events that follow one after another

PREVIOUS coming
before; earlier

RECRUITING asking people to
join a team or organization

SCHOLARSHIP money given
to a student to help pay
for schooling

STAMINA strength;
endurance; staying power

UNANIMOUS everyone
in agreement

UNIQUE one of a kind

DURABLE long lasting in
spite of much use or wear

DYNAMIC forceful and full
of energy

ELUSIVE having a quick
and clever ability to avoid
or escape

PARALYZED unable to feel
or use a part of the body

Index

About The Author

Mark Stewart grew up in New York City in the 1960s and 1970s– when the Mets, Jets, and Knicks all had championship teams. As a child, Mark read everything about sports he could lay his hands on. Today, he is one of the busiest sportswriters around. Since 1990, he has written close to 500 sports stories for kids, including profiles on more than 200 athletes, past and present. A graduate of Duke University, Mark served as senior editor of *Racquet*, a national tennis magazine, and was managing editor of *Super News*, a sporting goods industry newspaper. He is the author of every Grolier All-Pro Biography.